Diorama with Fleeing Figures

Merle Lyn Bachman

Diorama
with Fleeing Figures

Shearsman Books
Exeter

Published in the United Kingdom in 2009 by
Shearsman Books Ltd
58 Velwell Road
Exeter EX4 4LD

www.shearsman.com

ISBN   978-1-84861-012-5

Acknowledgements:

Some poems and earlier versions of poems in *Diorama with Fleeing Figures*
have been published by the following: *a.bacus* #97, *Antonym, Juxta* # 4, *The
Louisville Review*, *Outlet*, and *Syllogism* 3. Many thanks to all the editors.

Quotation marks in the poem 'Es brent zikh' indicate text drawn from
Isaac Babel, *1920 Diary,* edited by Carol J. Avins; translated by H. T. Willetts.
New Haven and London: Yale University Press, 1990.

Cover and all interior images copyright © Evan Siegel, 2009.

CONTENTS

This one's for Evan

UNDER THE FALLS

Every step beneath my feet splinters, threatens to cave.
Winds lash a throttled ship

—bald mountains saturated with rain
    distant fringe of remnant pine
white   pulse of   waterfall   beneath its veil we once sheltered
a century ago—

etched inside this wrist, scrimshaw

thorns stuck in the
basket of ribs   —cooled geode

Elected to this life, we ruled our minutes like petty
tyrants, not knowing
how they would rise against us.

—skull unearthed by the Sierra pine
the same
        as that one   scraped out of the mass grave
    half a world away.

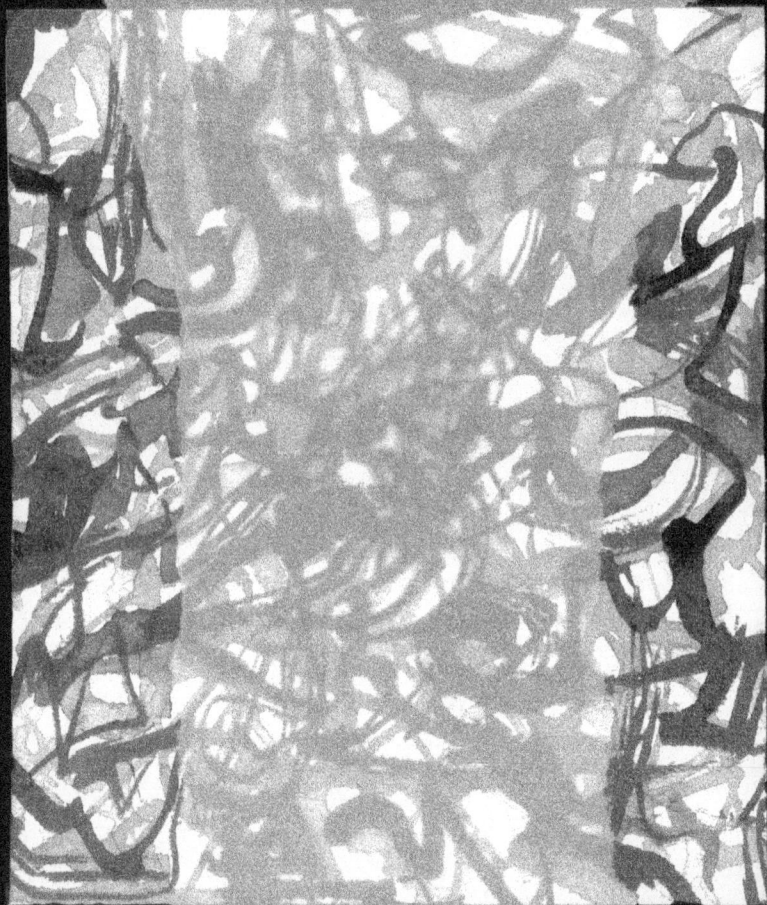

(THE BODY TELLS ITS STORY)

forgetting where, a lake,
   —on the dock where the wood felt warm at night
even though the air was cool. a function deep inside
the body, its branches   sheared

hard to be quiet enough, to hear: *shtil, sha, shtil*—

the warmth of enclosed regions. that primitive
animalism, emptying its spoon against the side of a dish
(calm as wires crossed.) an amusing puzzle,

like   ice in the upper peninsula—

a small dress of bone and pounded skin

the full range of motion

she keeps bleeding a clear sexual fluid
where is the location of desire?

untouched, it hangs   steep gradient cut loose this ridge

to drift   this many cloud unborn   seam

a supple call/caw

fields' blight the belly stalk

Peculiar gray-green day. the mind,   a smoke
    characteristics of   a frontal system

                                —startled awake

2 a.m. by dry lightning
thunder   again and again   not a drop of rain

—entered the village, noted scars of recent graves

—category 5 storm, approaching the lowlands

All that the eye can see, directly or via satellite.
days packed with tears, a woman's body its delicate
accord, the sensor picks up heat, alarms go off, he
"went off" & they fell like kindling, one by one

inside the most confused part of the forest.
we live in, live off   an architecture of the dead—
tools, songs, instructions, palpable material designed, handed
on, pulling the house around us its shell of concrete
dust, yes, the cherrywood furnishings the brick
ornament the stubborn
soiled pot

we enter the built world, roll into place
we carry on

when the girl walked
naked out of the field, they
photographed her

specificity of how my hands
hurt

tipped far back in the cup

making sense of what's "reported"
to consider   knowledge enough, just "knowing"

like clustered fruit
clinging to the ship's sides
smashed by the waves, tyrannical

waves begin as thoughts inside the mind
lightning exited her left foot
its sole

tell her Get out of the rain
say, The engines are all broken
Learn to live with history
—life jackets bobbing cherry-bright in the blue water
—children fixed at points, the lee shore another
woman's body

"movement of the subject
and of history" — what one presence added
briefly to the pine-tinged air

implanted with
experience, a kind of shrapnel

being female, being under
their watching

one more mind alert and not attached to anything
in a dark room surrounded by darkness

truant mountains running

I have this feeling of
no feeling

sometimes an engine falls off
or a wing

a quality of longing that cannot materialize
restricted from trees swaying, their bodies I used to sway
  in a long skirt,
willow leaves brushing the ground, a movement above my head
      like water
inviting me in, up   forward, their appetite and mine, birds
          slipping through

so he doesn't know, exactly, how you
got there or what time the region went
haywire. listening for telescopes, pulling
planets exacerbation of tendencies to
explode, be recorded

scanning the horizon for a temporary fate

trust. it all happens in silence
the bodies ant-like in their streaming towards the border
in the vacuum of the page we hear nothing
words an ornament
what we call "information"

in this realm, privacy resisted
was forced to pay. he doesn't know or
want to but the banners announce an end

white water breaking over bodies, the color "black" dissolved
by its assault

wanting not the same as having or reaching for degree.
unfolding in the sink
a curve of butter inside its dish
—what darkens in shut drawers
—what the linoleum covers

hands melt in the sun

—rim of the body
totalizing
what a man who had sworn to celibacy and complete
surrender wrote by a sputtering
light while the snow sifted through cracks
in his mountain temple: *this floating world*

"humans the only mammals whose breasts, continually
        swollen"
—shifting her body from leg to leg, trunk to trunk in
a series of choreographed
steps   the world's weight
pressed through her, locking
the drifting gate

Something snarled her hair
ripped the insides of her shoes right out

A cold wind found her at the edge of a road, where all roads led

Wrens like embers floated there

(This is where *body* becomes *forgetting*
Keep a diary of maps as if knowing exact
distance is the answer)

Warm places that unmake themselves, daily
and cause rescue workers to wear masks

On whose side is the woman on her side?
—heading upstream, gasping
into print

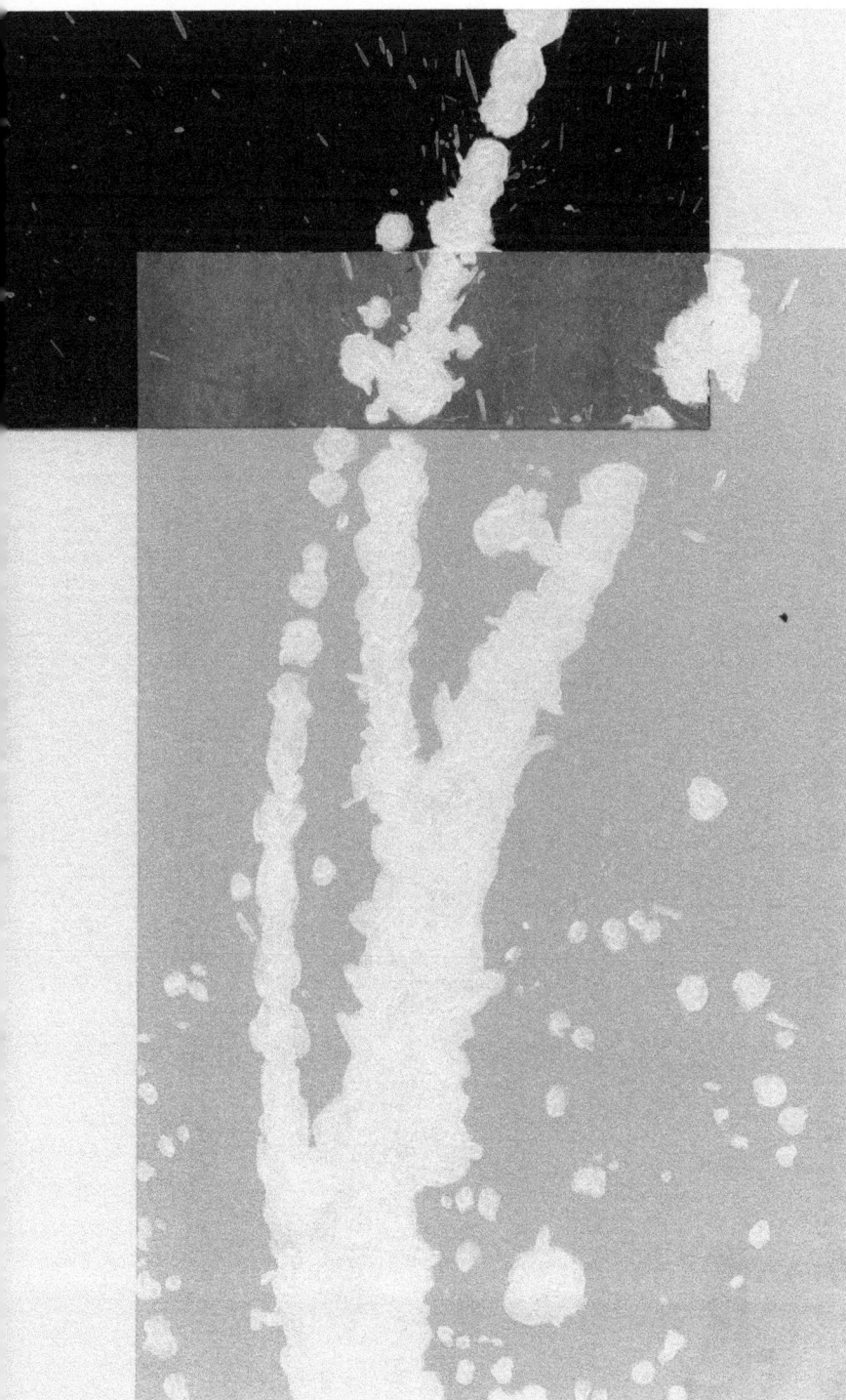

LONELY PLANET

small tunnels are rife & fill with vapors
pockets contain stalagmites
you can feel it if you stick your finger there
her fingers, like wands that have lost their magic.
through the lit glass of cafes

she asked for needles that would turn her
attention inward. stars topple from the Tour d'Eiffel
on a calendar nearby. empty plastic bottle purchased in
Tel Aviv in August 1998 says "Eden's Waters"
in Hebrew. this too has some significance
or she wouldn't have saved it, packed in various boxes and
moved from room to room, house to house.

hovering over

. . . the debris gets reabsorbed into the body, the tissues, linings, its
pockets, flaps, strings trailing, waving lazily in the molecular
breeze . . .

she keeps half-seeing: a flash of gold, a tail wriggling past;
hears sometimes
voices uttered by
mouths that are not there: murmurs, riddles, questionings
a rise and fall

brief lanterns on the swell

someone tells her: "learning of his brain tumor
put her breast cancer
into perspective"

the other's embrace: hot breath near your ear

inside one finds a number of city blocks, jammed together,
meters running empty, sour wind scraping
a violent   pavement

acreage you didn't know about: don't care to.

dreaming about the body can only harm you;
its funhouse of disappointments

in a world of survivors, the brave ride high
in tanks, bring *freedom*, a tasteless
colorless idea.

last night the wind scoured away snow
then rain came and further dissolved the crystalline mantle

maybe there's some hidden spot   an entirely
new territory   unexposed to the celestial light
of TV   where a small
band of us, unspoiled, begins
their day—with rituals of love, inexplicable
innocence. a place of no century, no national entity.

guidebooks issued to this region have blank pages
you read them and smile, tasting the distance   its safety
a country unlanguaged   only palace
nightingales, tinkling fountains   What humans
could stand to live in such a place

asleep on her chair, Vermeer's girl never
alters; though the viewer's hair has grayed, the painted-out
lover never bursts through the door.

why is it easier to clean and codify, separate, slip into
files, store away? the only logic, countering a growing disorder
whose roots snake everywhere. yet
orderliness works against voluptuous life.

a woman at the hair salon told her unexpectedly
the bad air in her neighborhood had given her fibroid
tumors; spoke quickly while running the credit card,
under her breath

the architecture of her own spine seems less
pointed, unstable; snow, falling through the branches
of the three-story oak, opposite the house.

plangent. its meaning escapes her, but her mouth
fills with its taste, a little
like blood.

listening to what might possibly be emptiness
takes courage.
(does emptiness have a sound?)

—and what she notices, whispers to herself
in trails around the house—
music stuck in her branches.

"we weren't meant to know so much
of the world," to feel so
helpless.
to carry with us that   constant failure

the student of a dying language, she must talk to herself
and even then
no one listens.

rife/roof

supple/stable/staple

ordinary detail as rescue.
graft of memories

the grifter—

so much hair cut off, she felt guilty

did they have to shave his head to do the surgery?
she has not written to him yet

staple

a woman she respected hissed "It's a death sentence" but really
she wants to know if the treatment
is working

stable

a handsome and talented man, for whom words exist in many
alphabets, luminous dimensions, and music is his mother tongue

apple

hurl it back at the maker, insist upon it:
we want out of this play!

no need to set the flaming sword at the gates

Eden's waters, a deceit
but the place
is real:
couched inside this body, this swirl of flesh:

pit-stop on the Ohio. night drugged black and shining.
they dragged the river for someone's body
a woman from the South, gone missing

but tonight's a picnic,
parked overlooking as snow
descends   drawn down by irreversible magnets
as if nothing that falls
could ever fly again

beauty has boldness
a certain   larval cold

pulling from the pit its light
carved into stone

pulling from the sorrowful its tinge
of happiness, in rivulets
over bone.

SHADOW SONG

slowly the shadow world gains
it seems not unusual to die, when half of life is "behind"
and a row of dark pines
trigger a revolving wind

★

trying to go backwards
uncoiling the hard work
cricket sound suspended like audible jewels
darkness paints the inside of every hull
restless volumes shifting under ground
a woman lays her head upon her hand at the rich table, sleeps
no one knows the figure at the open door
the artist changed his mind, submerged it under glowing paints
we want to sleep and not be bothered by this
dream and press our hands into the walls
making happiness is the opposite of vanishing
unsettled, pull up to the island, its copious ghosts
reflected; sink; wait

Gathering courage to remember
lost languages—
scooped from the guts of a ripened pear.

Pliant
stripes fall
pull the surface towards you

but past the left shoulder, a blackened ember
the owl clipped in its beak when it was fire

also the outline of a mountain, basalt and snow, its peak
glittering.

Harm done   the harm done
threatening like wings, centered over a horizon.
The river fans before entering the sea, deposits its wealth
in centuries.

A small cusp of   land   retains grace
where you slept, afraid of   actual creatures   real fangs

Inside these tableaux
nothing real exists
but thoughts — a small brush fire — an absence of hands.

Shtetl Photographs

di layt   di kindershe layt

   what is lazy about these   washings?
a *zumer tog*, a summer day in

april

from a window, see the young ones, their jackets
vanished
the skin, pale   oral and blooming
   distinct

pushing (wheeling) a barrow

who is a tired *meydl*, her mouth of   fur?

small circles, on black and white
   squares
with inches   of gray: photographs

(touching knees under the table
(the lamplight makes   a wedge

a town, its many   heads
a pool of knowledge

who led them (pallor)   into the woods (a blur)
one day?

what is the lifted   edge

its blush
that soaks through—   ?

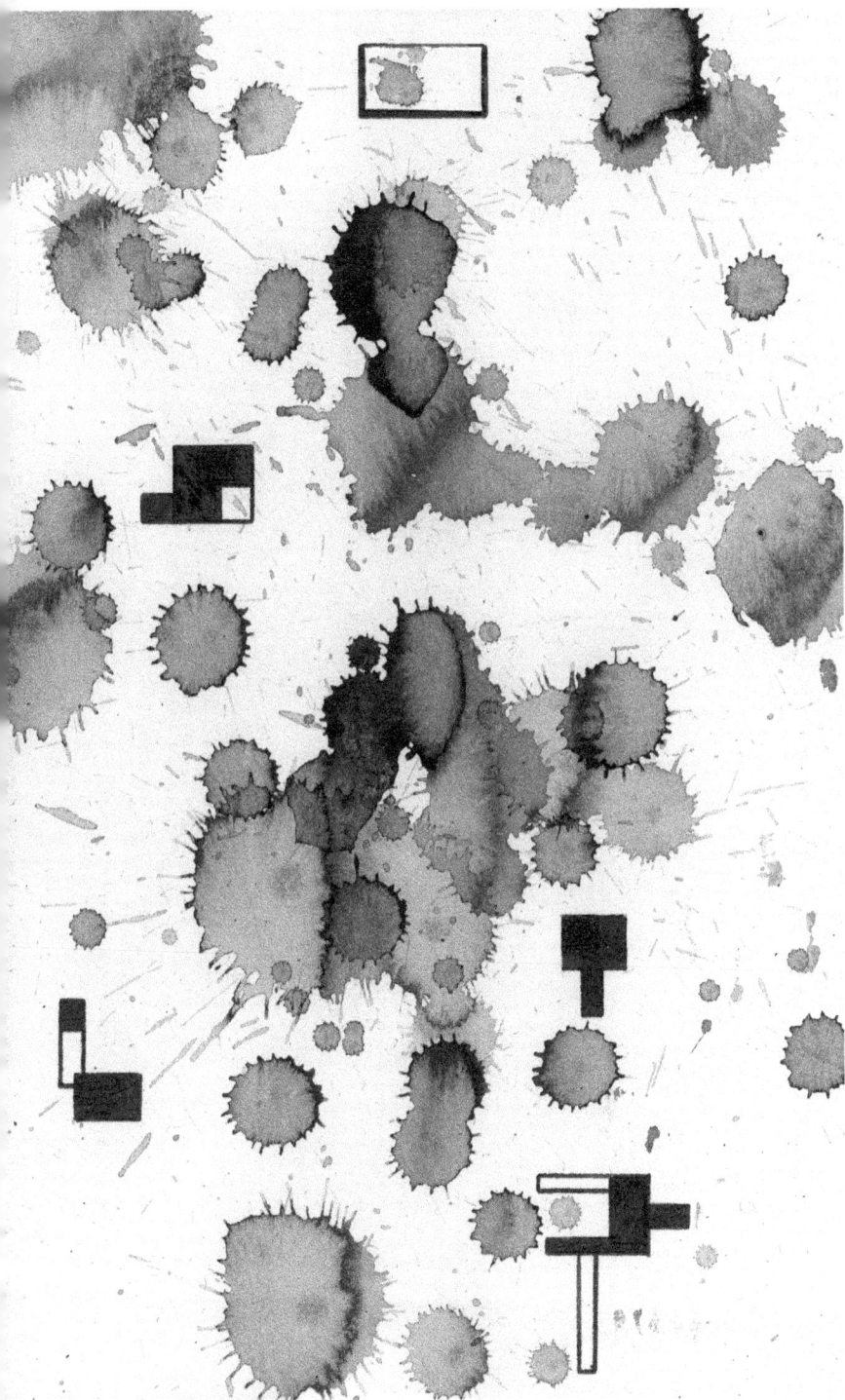

Fragments – from the Black Forest
(drawing upon the Brothers Grimm and a Yiddish primer)

The movements of swallows control our thoughts.

Ice forms in the small of the back, the windows fall to pieces
    like marzipan,
lilies interwoven in the lattices, a tower deserted for years and
    inside
a sleeping monument
(lips half-open).

★

—thicket of dark

a gallop of   ravens   to regiment the quest

small, a plunder   (stationed in the forest)

tiny in wallow
my horse drifts along like thistledown

to line tunics to line

spectral moment: one of them cracked, blood poured out,
pitiful.

"To illustrate present tense of verbs with prefixes when
modified by an adverb, use the example: <u>I do not question</u>"

Open!

Get up!

Cease!

What are the imperatives of
cherries?

Sample sentence:
*My uncle rode to Germany many years ago, and there he bought for us
many beautiful things.*

And again:

*Can you speak German, Jacob? No, I cannot;
I speak Yiddish only.*

a twig
towards evening
berry

An orientation towards open fields, despite the closed circle
of a little town. At the edges one has to pass with caution, the
place swarming with bent shapes. *My teacher said that all
Jewish children must know how to read, write and speak
Yiddish.* Before the word for "town," the word for "words"
(warm and dark). Something chases
after them.

Sample sentence:
Dora, will you go with us to the forest today?
I will not go to the forest with you.

Sitting in his room, reading; *be still.* Wrens revolve around
the painted house. Accused
of lying, but summer is near, and
     The children are sitting in the yard, singing a lovely song.

A small knife came from long ago.

Sleep, my little ones: farmakht di eygelekh

_____ *your tender little eyes.*   In the two hundred
and thirtieth street, a white house, a tower, a river brings fish
to the door. Its silver is heavy.

What is prettier, warmer, lazier? We are ashamed
to tell you.   He catches me, and I give him
my shirt

Laughter of bread and milk
"To run" sounds like *float*

The pitcher goes to the well till one day   it breaks

Scattered like crumbs from the pocket of a heavy coat.
in summer, a soft turn under moist stars. stains on his shirt
from sleeping in the field.   to burst out, undress. raisins.

     questions in the present tense
modified.

(an archivist interrupts:

She cannot read

the curlicues and flowers of the *hentshrift,* their writing, *Yidishe*
    reyzlekh, the roses
stuffed in pockets wadded into walls, pulled forth   delicately

from a pocked and rusted milk-can:)

We wanted to write you a letter, but we could not.

(she notes:

—Every story has the same ending:
  "and then they were shot.")

Hunger for strawberries

kissed to the river

  pulling till the muscles shone

a smashed-pot sound   rice inside sheets   until the man's head

  floated to the surface

familiar as   inside a stick of wood

  a smell like thunder

loop of stunned desire

    jackdaw in angel rites

a spangle before guns

    real tears the statue wept

in robes buffeted by someone's last cries

shot through with potatoes   a great wheel

of laughter

ravens stuffed

with corn & glitter

The wicked strong wind is whistling
and the poor leaves have no rest.

A Few Words from the Future

Warm summer breath bending the long grass of a field
    an old barn filled with dust, owl's nests

  broken mug cracked dish stained mirror

   elements that spell a past beyond field, or house, beyond
state lines, turnpike, scrawled edge of coast, rushing over
    vast water   to an older country
   where these things were made
   where the owners of these things once lived

To talk with people who carried with them over water

   pure forms from their old life: book. candlestick.   dish.

here, given soil they planted
rhubarb beans peas corn
protected hatchlings under a zigzag roof
and in their heads a language few remember

Abandoned field   tingling with practices left fallow:

how simply we are converted   from whole to part

to limb, to bone

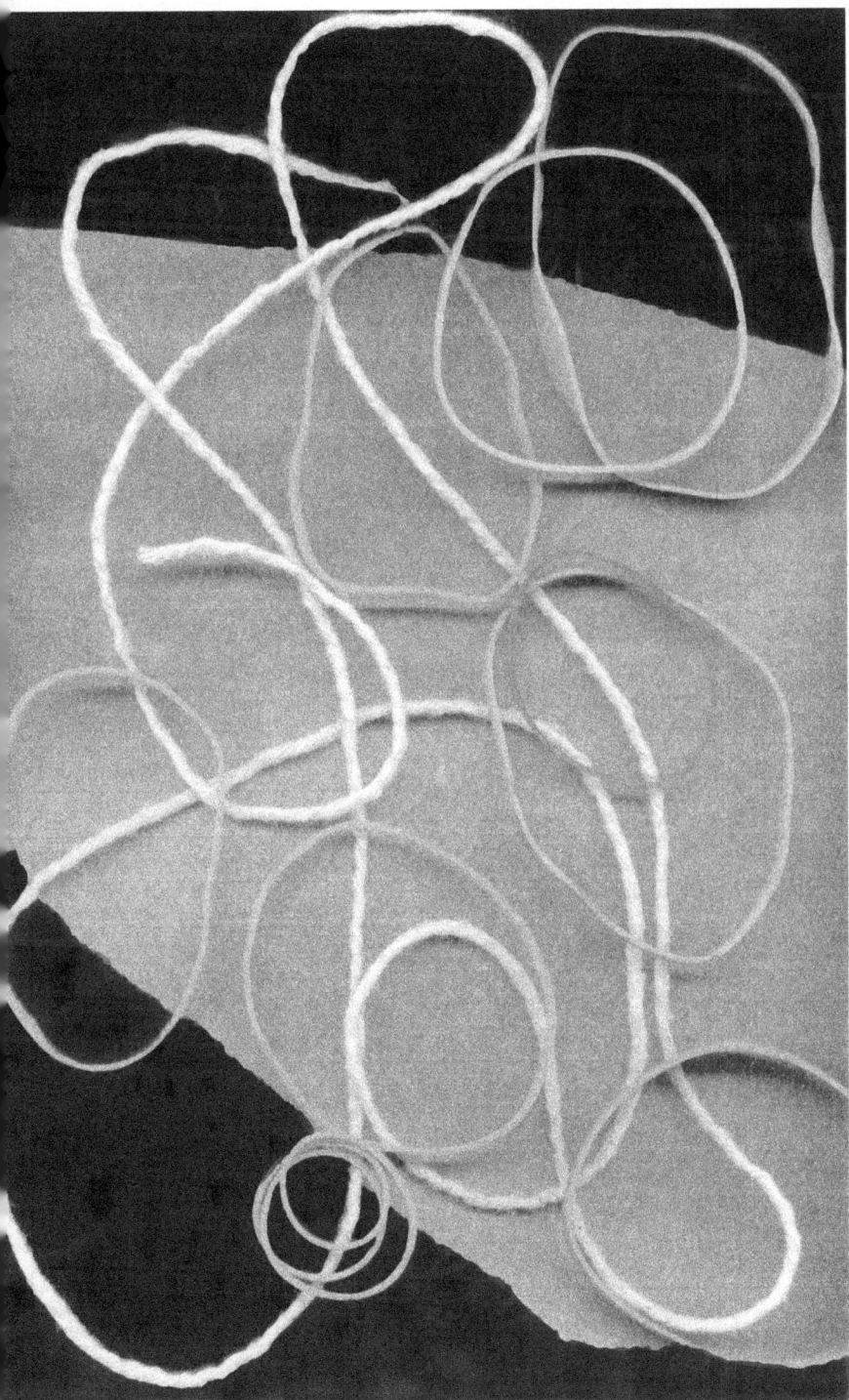

Es Brent Zikh
(from Isaac Babel's *1920 Diary*)

Inexplicable the man "attached" to army's flank
a spy who fluctuates, learns clatter of light wounds
a taste in the mouth preceding aeroplane
explosion occupational
hazard "tea with milk is made, Ivan goes for sugar machine gun
       fire"

jam

cottage in the forest, when sleeping [no identity] Russian or
       Cossack or

A sad country   they hid their horses quietly
  with weeping women

a smell of legless
wheat fields
volumes tumbled out amid the order
—changed hands   (m)issing page(s)

the rain but bloodless, plowed
her wasted beauty could not blemish
or stop if she wanted to

fresh apples, a bridle
the filth of shape

"—I am giving (misreading: *given*) milk—"

describe humiliation. stunted. cut-off
talk of widows — fried eggs — new cemetery —
promise sugar, abandon carts

narrow-chested drop of blood left

horses, stupid-looking. bone of exchange
creaking
pigs too sticky
in velvet caps
"all Galicia infected"
find a bed, bore into it

a cage inside the house, packed blue with stars

in the distance wet fields   August heat
fall liquid smarts the skin
eyes with echoes   terrible no treatment
mourned all night cherry tea I was deprived of

"on the fringe of the forest"
blueing, whiteing

troops advance bayonets under
swarm of fell
bombs, five, six in a minute

—the edges of centuries interpenetrated—

toward sour seclusion   myriads
   looting biography

torpid remount   "To horse"   under the shadow of flight

sleep wandering around
pluck hay from head

"what a beautiful and necessary thing is rest"

enveloped in

smoke, disaster lamps threshed by grief

insects kill thick mist, its rumbling

with an unripe Jew, all horses

impassable—

building torched

. . . *stop*   *sleep*   *stars* . . .

The Burning

sharp premonitions occupy a discordant field

the January light is turning to snow

there are figures escaping a luminous background

their names are hidden, stuffed inside their mouths

hard bits of white afternoon

all the red life locked in fleeing people

avenues blocked by stalled equipment

guns leveled over roof edges

a noise enters history   registers
as final

the town   one of a dozen in their part of Europe

the year, memorized by students even now

sitting at small desks fighting

to stay awake

AMSTERDAM

desire collects and hugs itself, snug

carpets alloyed with velvet flowers

red spills forth from the earth, scrawls myriad names across
pavement

there are clocks that count backwards the time remaining
until you retire

but no one really knows how much time remains

& so bicycles clatter over four hundred-year-old streets

attended by ghosts clad in cheerful flesh, hair and smoke

light bursts

over the squatting houses

in a few minutes it will have vanished

so utterly even memory can't revive it

but desire hurtles herself forward (assuming a gender)

unbuttons from crumbs of winter soil

moldy smell of stale socks, unwashed cups in the kitchen

stained lampshades and yarn pictures

smudged photographs of strangers

desire tips herself always toward *horizon*

according to no timetable   filed under no   subject heading

but we give names to things:
stars   weapons   products   man-and-wife

naming, claiming

The Dutch painted women writing   or reading letters

absorbed in the nakedly private act

under sensitive lemon light   in cool blue-tiled rooms

paint's density teaching   interiority

lead white leading   to a kind of madness   and vermillion?
    ochre?

teaching us   to imagine a shielded love

cast in a forehead's ivory   never revealed but   suggested

by the hand grasping cream paper

the tremble of a pen

as a pearl glistens among honeycombs

the body's tender lockets   contain surprises

and a girl, sleeping in the 17th century, can suggest
a contemporary world

"days spent writing a good sentence"

he leans over her lightly, the letter's never finished,
   always being written

the peculiar tint of winter light, viewed from a southeasterly point

amid bare brick, the trees' stark arrangement of pale limbs

house jacketed with cold. flames in the chimney

pictorial highlights embossed in foil

a stone's throw into a stone. a hinge opens   a chest—

but this architecture   confuses

so it's best to forget the pelvic rim, natural lock

of the pubis

in Amsterdam you find yourself

alone   pulses thin and fluttery

like water in the lower strata of a creek

a mere splash at its origins, soaking moss under crust
of February ice

waiting for   uncoiling   the setting-in-motion

ABANDONING JERUSALEM

Sky the only thing that never changed,

she fixed on it   but why the same word, *rimon*, for
    pomegranate, grenade

lemons cut open to suck through sugared lips?

a particular fate (met in the bomb shelter), still hovering

in Zion Square

an instant 30 years ago revised (just the context

that changes), bauble on the bench, package of oranges,
    converted from

fruit to incendiary device, hurtle in the crowd-flow, abandoned

refrigerator, suspicious objects, *hefetz*, thing, a thing

of desiring

long legs that reached   to the end of the bed

so perfect, she thinks, with cats squalling and thick
fragrance of wild roses

man with a frozen hip from the war, occasional casings from
spent bullets marked "*alef*"

buildings erected on those fields, goats gone, when he says *ani
gomer* "I'm coming" it's the same as to *finish, finish-off*

the most innocent sentences grow cold; the light
drains out of them.

dreamed I had to go back, through endless corridors marked
terminal and no fresh air. tickets could not be revoked.
on the #9 bus heading through 100 Gates, a package
tucked to a man's chest like a baby.
carrying nervous collapse in the pit
of my stomach, even under bright tarp of sun.

at the Wall, ugly stones fringed with bits of paper. the most
intense wishes, wedged
inside cracks. we back up to show respect. soldiers search
my bags, touching
everything. I get on the bus

reproduction of a voice amplified in the evening gloom
keens a familiar language

thin cirrus, a glitter in the air—
mirage of a living sea in the distance, pasted over the dead one.

  recalling
a phosphor that washes up nights on Tel Aviv beaches
—the same moon, wrapped in white *hijab*

how difficult to wear that shade of sky
or the smoke, caught in twisted branches

At a table in downtown Jerusalem
under lights that bead a private garden with eccentric color.

it's damp and the walls black from years of diesel soot.
We used to study yoga in an empty building not far
from here, it alternated as

a bomb shelter. afraid to take the city buses, we walk
everywhere until
feet ache. if only

we could sit outside the city gates
under the shade
of a little gourd tree

Thirty years ago the man puffed his pipe furiously
in the living room of a house in the German colony
(the Palestinians fled in '48)
where we sat, students sipping tea and pretending
to sophistication.

The settlers are right, the land is ours.
a moment: its crest: it gently passed.

Now

   empty bulbs tip   up   flare north
and revisions begin, a mottling   deep inside skin

            the "settlers" with watered lawns swimming pools terra
cotta pastiche   beneath their vines and fig trees   and
            careful watch of IDF
            soldiers who protect their luxuriant
                    disregard

the ranks break, right and left   scattered in wide-angle march
so many breaths
would deafen except
for the roar of metal parts   grinding and crushing tender earth
beneath

and olive trees   caught up in the jaws   —some houses
crammed
      with family belongings
  —sometimes an invalid who
can't escape

Accustomed to the sound of low-flying planes
the view she cherished

unsafe to walk or drive in

a spice added to hanging wash

not a pinpoint for a sniper but his body
saves her, not categorized as
disaster, shirts made of bullets, what

happened then

still happens now, the point of thinking may be

to remember chance encounters
rearrangements split

open in a dripping garden

No Evil Eye

bronchial roses
fistfuls of light

streets reassume a prior status
the eyes of statues moisten
in advance

sitting on a mountain of   shadow
lifted   a place I used to dream   stupefied
happiness

the insides of my eyelids flower red—
waiting inside each face

on the # 9 bus
from downtown Jerusalem

crushed velvet   translations

In the Memory Room

kind edges. eggs frying, carpets pulled back, an intrusion
of fog. where we are at this moment—by the kitchen sink.
a sack of Pilgrim flour.
dried roses, stubbed-out.
skin sticky with blanket.
as secret as sex, stuffed in bags of night, the lock's tongue
lengthening inside the door—

what the left shoulder carries, hunched in its adhesions.
headaches, tapping open a blank gate.
hair falling on a porcelain surface.
longing, a mistake
carried over like a number added wrong,
column to column, in the old days.
the difference between then and now.
an adaptation, trimmed with dull shears.

inside the New York State museum, the only breather amid

the dioramas: reading the displays, geological strata, Indian

longhouses lit by shaded bulbs, glowing waxen eyes. perhaps here

on the skeleton of State Street, the butter

peddler roamed, carrying

a faint light. old married couples tucked into Dutch

beds, they met

at the teawater pump, filled their urns with

each other's love. the rhythmic mating

of cobblestone and horse's hoof. tell it to the smudged

cascade, forms like silkworms

winding through the streets. it's the infant funeral

procession, and men are dressed in christening

gowns, spitting up tears and milk.

first there was the Ice Age, then the hunters then the longhouse
then the Dutch the settlers and redcoats then the wars then people
on ships, moving upriver with peddler-packs, bathhouses on Ferry
Street where years later my father's father ran his numbers, died
sitting in the *shvitz*, a towel on his lap.

my father's father and his father before him. dark-skinned from
Odess, a gangster there in natty jacket and cuffs. my mother's
mother and her mother before her. digging *bulbes* in Soroki,
losing track of dirty children.

the break-up of our floe: splintered bodies of ships, a living
cargo suspended below decks slick with vomit and filth. the trees
felled in distant forests to build those ships; the peasants who
lived deep in those woods; their dull hatchets.
their eyes' cold shine.

we forgot to ask about the songs, stitched inside a shirt with
        stolen eggs.

rhymes scratched beneath a lid in blue. the children's chant bent

under a bucket's weight, miles in winter (even the *goyishe* children
        knew Yiddish).

we want to hear the hiss on frosty nights, a samovar or snow
        that hits

the grate, or the breath between your teeth.

and now it's someone else's history, where embroidery

catches in the throat. a sooty corner, darkening. feral

tongues, twitching among branches.

glue on, then, in strips of sentences, the long brocade.

horse's canter in a frozen field.

a blanket rubbed with stars, a coffin

a shoe, bleached wood, a ship, ice in the channel breaks

a mouth opens: a wooden boat, lined with fleece
a word lining—

mocking-up a word-child:
barest knuckle, sack of wind

a crow moves in the landscape   ink blot

on chimney

radiant alcoves

mouths moving, speaking lines
of something before a flood
tears them away   a translation not yet
written in its original language

unlatched, voluble, fed by hidden springs, a jammed door lifts
completely off its hinges

blankening space, far-off   smell of exposed roots
before the rising waters
cover them—